PRESENTED TO:

____

FROM:

____

DATE:

____

WHO I AM

WHO I AM

REBORN AND CERTIFIED IN CHRIST

Terry Nichols-Alexander

JL Holman
a division of MEI
Visalia, California

Published by JL Holman
P.O. Box 6602, Visalia, CA 93290
http://www.jlholman.com

a division of MEI

Cover design: Lisa Thomson

ISBN 978-1-893995-14-7

Printed in the United States of America

DEDICATION

GOD
Who saw the need in me first to come into the
knowledge of who I am in Christ Jesus.

My daughter, TaShauna Nichols and my son, RaShaun Nichols

My Grandchildren:
Know that the truth is available to you at your early age and on a level
that is conducive to your understanding. The Holy Spirit will meet you
where you are in your search.
Emari Breauna, Deaunte' Larenz, Antonio Jones,
Makayla, Zakyyah, and RaShaun D. Jr.

My mother, Hattie Flowers, who for two and
half plus years provided shelter and supported me.

Using the Interactive Devotional

This devotional provides a workbook aspect that is divided into sections with each section containing 12 weeks of declarations.

Take your time to study, meditate, and rewrite the scriptures and declarations as you make each one personal to you.

Before starting this 60-week journey, pray and ask Father God to help you understand and retain the scriptures. As you do this daily, the word of God will begin to transform your mind and when problems or situations arise, the Holy Spirit will remind you of God's word.

Use the following steps:
1. Read each scripture out loud at least three times.
2. Rewrite the scriptures to make it personal to you.
3. Read the revision with your name out loud at least three times.
4. Throughout the day continue to quote the scriptures (using your name).
5. At the end of the day, write your reflections concerning the scripture(s).
6. Before turning in for the night, write a personal prayer about the scripture(s) you've been meditating on.

CONTENTS

ACKNOWLEDGEMENT

I appreciate all family members who provided spiritual support, encouragement, inspiration, prayer, material needs and medical support, as well as, contributed to the completion of this book: Marilyn Nichols, Lisa Crawford, and Ruby Jewel Nichols.

My spiritual family: Pastor Willie G. Nutt, initially introduced me to Christ Jesus and who led me to give my life to Christ. Pastor Nutt taught me so much about Christ, and in such a way that I wanted to know more and form a relationship that was personal.

Pastor Janice Holman: Not only is she my spiritual sister but my teacher and my publisher. Without her involvement and encouragement and prayers, only God knows if this would be a reality.

Pastors' Larry and Leslie Toliver: They have been a constant source of prayer, encouragement, inspiration and unconditional love.

Friends who encouraged, inspired, prayed and believed in me through it all: I want to assure you that I have not forgotten the kind words of encouragement, support and inspiration that you blessed me with to move forward, and to continue with my assignment, while not being dismayed by the hindrances and delays that seemed never-ending.

Thank you for your never-ending prayers: Candace Forbes, Timothy Finley, Isaac Langford, Lily Thompson, and my spiritual family at San Jose Word of Faith Christian Center and Abundant Life Christian Center Fellowship.

Finally, Alexia Perschmann, a cab driver in Minnesota, who without her intervention, I wouldn't be here today. I thank God for our exchange while I was visiting in Minnesota.

Rebirth:

The action of reappearing or starting to flourish or increase after a decline; revival. Experiencing a complete spiritual change.

Certified:

Officially recognize (someone or something) as possessing certain qualifications or meeting certain standards.

BELIEVERS CAN, IN FAITH, LEGALLY DECLARE THE WRITTEN DECREE (GOD'S WORD) AND BECOME TRANSFORMED BY THE RENEWING OF THEIR MINDS. WE WILL HAVE WHAT WE DECLARE!

INTRODUCTION

Father God has declared over hundreds of decrees regarding the believer's identity and the reality of our existence (purpose) on this earth, as a believer in Jesus Christ.

Decree: "A formal and authoritative order, especially one having the force of law."

Declare: "To say something in a solemn and empathetic manner; acknowledge possession of; to announce, reveal or express."

The above definitions demonstrate God's perspective of what He has spoken as legal and binding. The rebirth is a "guaranteed new life" in Christ and made possible by the love of God for us. He gave up his only son and the son gave up his life for us, so that we could be reunited with Father God. We can now start life over. God has provided us with a blueprint of how we are supposed to live, and a guide to help us get it right along the way.

As you read and speak each decree, in faith, understand that this is what God has said about you. So make each scripture personal to you. Allow the Holy Spirit to reveal the Word to you in terms you understand. He will meet you at your level of knowledge and faith. Romans 10:8 says, "The word is near you, even in your mouth and in your heart; that is the Word of Faith which we preach." We are told in Romans 10:9, "confess with our mouth and believe in our hearts"—this is the basis of faith. Faith is required when declaring the word of God: speak, believe and receive what God has already given and prepared for you through Christ.

Understand that faith doesn't come over night. The "word" is like a "seed". It must first be planted in your heart, and watered. Memorizing and studying the Word helps to plant it into your heart. The watering comes when you meditate on the Word day and night, and allow the Holy Spirit to lead you into an understanding of that Word.

My relationship with the Lord has grown and developed over the past seven years into an unbreakable bond that I cannot do without! His undeniable presence is refreshing and comforting amongst so many other things. God is everything we need daily! Remember, God told Moses to tell the people that His name is "I AM, THAT I AM".

In 2014, I began to suffer from seizures—since I don't have epilepsy in my family—the doctors, to date, are not able to determine the cause of them. I was experiencing six seizures a day. The medications caused me to feel like the "walking dead", in addition to the other adverse physical side effects. It was through all the chaos and trials that I realized His presence was with me! I made the choice to stand on my faith in God's healing by declaring the Word of God over every situation, and it changed for my good and God's glory. He turned things around and healed me. You see, God's Word and authority has been decreed and declared since the beginning of time. When we declare the Word of God in our situations, believing what we say, with expectation, we will see it come to past.

This book is designed to help you recognize who you are as a child of God. As you read and meditate on the scriptures, make the scripture personal by rewriting it with your name. Take the time to not only declare who you are, but study the scriptures related to each declaration so you might "grow in the grace and in the knowledge of our Lord and Savior Jesus Christ." (2 Peter 3:18)

Terry Nichols-Alexander

SECTION I
Weeks 1-12

Faith comes by hearing, and hearing by the word of God.
(ROMANS 10:17)

I am Abraham's Offspring

And if ye be Christ's, then are ye Abraham's seed, and heirs
according to the promise.
Galatians 3:29 KJV

I am Free

So if the Son makes you free, you will be free indeed.
John 8:36 NASB

I am Abundantly filled

The thief does not come except to steal, and to kill, and to destroy. I have come that they
may have life, and that they may have it more abundantly.
John 10:10 NKJV

Reflections

Prayer

I am a Child of God

The Spirit Himself bears witness with our spirit that we are children of God.
Romans 8:6 NKJV

___

___

___

I am God's possession

*Who (Jesus) gave himself for us to redeem us from all lawlessness and to purify for himself
a people for his own possession who are zealous for good works.*
Titus 2:14 ESV

___

___

___

I am Standing

*By whom also we have access by faith into this grace wherein we stand, and rejoice
in hope of the glory of God.*
Romans 5 :2 KJV

___

___

___

Reflections

Prayer

I am a Son of God

For as many as are led by the Spirit of God, they are the sons of God.
Romans 8:14 KJV

I am Abounding in hope

Now the God of hope fill you with all joy and peace in believing, that ye may abound in hope, through the power of the Holy Ghost.
Romans 15:13 KJV

I am Freely given all things

He (God) who did not spare His own Son, but delivered Him over for us all, how will He not also with Him freely give us all things?
Romans 8:32 NASB

Reflections

Prayer

Reflections

I am Light

Then Jesus spoke to them again, saying, "I am the light of the world. He who follows Me shall not walk in darkness, but have the light of life."
John 8:12 NKJV

I am Possessor of All things

So let no one boast in men. For all things are yours, whether Paul or Apollos or Cephas or the world or life or death or the present or the future—all are yours, and you are Christ's, and Christ is God's.
1 Corinthians 3:21-23 ESV

I am His Soldier

Thou therefore endure hardness, as a good soldier of Jesus Christ. No man that warreth entangleth himself with the affairs of this life; that he may please him who hath chosen him to be a soldier.
2 Timothy 2:3-4 KJV

Reflections

Prayer

I am Able

I can do all things through Christ which strengtheneth me.
Philippians 1:13 KJV

I am Gifted

Since we have gifts that differ according to the grace given to us, each of us is to exercise them accordingly: if prophecy, according to the proportion of his faith.
Romans 12:6 NASB

I am Given magnificent promises

For by these He has granted to us His precious and magnificent promises, so that by them you may become partakers of the divine nature, having escaped the corruption that is in the world by lust.
2 Peter 1:4 NASB

Reflections

Prayer

I am a Conqueror

Nay, in all these things we are more than conquerors through him that loved us.
Romans 8:37 KJV

I am Flowing with Life

He who believes in Me, as the Scripture has said, out of his heart will flow rivers of living water."
John 7:38 NKJV

I am Jesus' Glorious body

Who will transform our lowly body to be like his glorious body, by the power that enables him even to subject all things to himself.
Philippians 3:21 *ESV*

Reflections

Prayer

I am Filled with God's power

*But you will receive power when the Holy Spirit has come upon you, and you will be
my witnesses in Jerusalem and in all Judea and Samaria, and to the end of the earth.*
Acts 1:8 ESV

I am Standing firm

Now he which stablisheth us with you in Christ, and hath anointed us, is God.
2 Corinthians 1:21 KJV

I am a Good person

The steps of a good man are ordered by the Lord: and he delighteth in his way.
Psalm 37:23 KJV

Reflections

Prayer

I am Abounding in grace

And God is able to make all grace abound toward me; that I, always having all sufficiency in all things, may abound to every good work.
2 Corinthians 9:8 KJV

I am Abounding in Abundance

The thief cometh not, but for to steal, and to kill, and to destroy: I am come that they might have life, and that they might have it more abundantly.
John 10:10 KJV

I am Given His Holy Spirit

Who also sealed us and gave us the Spirit in our hearts as a pledge.
2 Corinthians 1:22 NASB

Reflections

Prayer

I am Glorified with Him

*It was for this He called you through our gospel, that you may gain the glory of
our Lord Jesus Christ.*
2 Thessalonians 2:14 NASB

I am God's Gift to Christ

*Father, I desire that they also, whom You have given Me, be with Me where I am, so
that they may see My glory which You have given Me, for You loved Me before the
foundation of the world.*
John 17:24 NASB

I am Watered

*The Lord will guide you continually, And satisfy your soul in drought, And
strengthen your bones; You shall be like a watered garden, And like
a spring of water. whose waters do not fail.*
Isaiah 58:11 NKJV

Reflections

Prayer

Reflections

I am a Living stone

You also, as living stones, are being built up a spiritual house, a holy priesthood, to offer up spiritual sacrifices acceptable to God through Jesus Christ.
1 Peter 2:5 NKJV

I am the Lord's

*One will say, 'I am the Lord's'; Another will call himself by the name of Jacob;
Another will write with his hand, 'The Lord's,' And name
himself by the name of Israel.*
Isaiah 44:5 NKJV

I am given Power

*And he called the twelve together and gave them power and authority over
all demons and to cure diseases.*
Luke 9:1 ESV

Reflections

Prayer

I am Helped

*So that we may boldly say, The Lord is my helper, and I will
not fear what man shall do unto me.*
Hebrews 13:6 KJV

I am Prepared for glory

*In order to make known the riches of his glory for vessels of mercy, which he has
prepared beforehand for glory.*
Romans 9:23 ESV

I am Strengthened in Him

*That he would grant you, according to the riches of his glory, to be strengthened with
might by his Spirit in the inner man.*
Ephesians 3:16 KJV

Reflections

Prayer

I am Abundantly Supplied

*But I have all, and abound: I am full, having received of Epaphroditus the things
which were sent from you, an odour of a sweet smell, a sacrifice acceptable,
well pleasing to God.*
Philippians 4:18 KJV

I am Sustained

*By thee have I been holden up from the womb: thou art he that took me out of my
mother's bowels: my praise shall be continually of thee.*
Psalm 71:6 KJV

I am a Temple

*Know ye not that ye are the temple of God, and that the Spirit of God
dwelleth in you?*
1 Corinthians 3:16 KJV

Reflections

Prayer

SECTION II
Weeks 13-24

We have the mind of Christ.
(1 CORINTHIANS 2:16)

I am Accepted

*To the praise of the glory of his grace, wherein he hath made
us accepted in the beloved.*
Ephesians 1:6 KJV

I am Accessible to God

For through him we both have access by one Spirit unto the Father.
Ephesians 2:18 KJV

I am Adequate

*Not that we are sufficient of ourselves to think anything as of ourselves;
but our sufficiency is of God.*
2 Corinthians 3:5 KJV

Reflections

Prayer

I Am is for me

*What then shall we say to these things? If God is for us,
who is against us?*
Romans 8:31 NASB

I am Gracious

He who loves purity of heart And whose speech is gracious, the king is his friend.
Proverbs 22:11 NASB

I am Granted grace in Christ

*For if by the transgression of the one, death reigned through the one, much more those
who receive the abundance of grace and of the gift of righteousness will reign in life through
the One, Jesus Christ. The Law came in so that the transgression would increase; but
where sin increased, grace abounded all the more.*
Romans 5:17, 20 NASB

Reflections

Prayer

I Am Loved

For God so loved the world that He gave His only begotten Son, that whoever believes in Him should not perish but have everlasting life.
John 3:16 NKJV

I am Made by God

Know that the Lord, He is God; It is He who has made us, and not we ourselves; We are His people and the sheep of His pasture.
Psalm 100:3 NKJV

I am a Magnifier of God

I will praise the name of God with a song, And will magnify Him with thanksgiving.
Psalm 69:30 NKJV

Reflections

Prayer

I Am Protected

*Because he holds fast to me in love, I will deliver him; I will protect him,
because he knows my name.*
Psalm 91:14 ESV

I am Provided for

*But seek first the kingdom of God and his righteousness, and all these
things will be added to you.*
Matthew 6:33 ESV

I am Thought about

*How precious also are thy thoughts unto me, O God! how great is the sum of them! If
I should count them, they are more in number than the sand: when I awake,
I am still with thee.*
Psalm 139:17-18 KJV

Reflections

Prayer

I Am Transferred into His Kingdom

*Who hath delivered us from the power of darkness, and hath translated us into
the kingdom of his dear Son.*
Colossians 1:13 KJV

I am Transformed

*But we all, with open face beholding as in a glass the glory of the Lord, are changed
into the same image from glory to glory, even as by the Spirit of the Lord.*
2 Corinthians 3:18 KJV

I am Adopted

*Having predestinated us unto the adoption of children by Jesus Christ to himself,
according to the good pleasure of his will.*
Ephesians 1:5 KJV

Reflections

Prayer

Reflections

I Am Alive with Christ

Even when we were dead in sins, hath quickened us together with
Christ, (by grace ye are saved;).
Ephesians 2:5 KJV

I am Guarded by God

For this reason I also suffer these things, but I am not ashamed; for I know whom I
have believed and I am convinced that He is able to guard what
I have entrusted to Him until that day.
2 Timothy 1:12 NASB

I am Guarded by God's peace

And the peace of God, which surpasses all comprehension, will guard your hearts
and your minds in Christ Jesus.
Philippians 4:7 NASB

Reflections

Prayer

I Am Sealed

In Him you also trusted, after you heard the word of truth, the gospel of your salvation; in whom also, having believed, you were sealed with the Holy Spirit of promise.
Ephesians 1:13 NKJV

I am Guaranteed

In Him, you also, after listening to the message of truth, the gospel of your salvation—having also believed, you were sealed in Him with the Holy Spirit of promise, who is given as a pledge of our inheritance, with a view to the redemption of God's own possession, to the praise of His glory.
Ephesians 1:13-14 NASB

I am a Member of Christ's body

For we are members of His body, of His flesh and of His bones.
Ephesians 5:30 NKJV

Reflections

Prayer

I Am Powerful in God

Behold, I give you the authority to trample on serpents and scorpions, and over all the power of the enemy, and nothing shall by any means hurt you.
Luke 10:19 NKJV

I am Purchased

And they sang a new song, saying, "Worthy are you to take the scroll and to open its seals, for you were slain, and by your blood you ransomed people for God from every tribe and language and people and nation.
Revelation 5:9 ESV

I am Renewing my mind

For "who has known the mind of the Lord that he may instruct Him?" But we have the mind of Christ.
1 Corinthians 2:16 NKJV

Reflections

Prayer

I Am Purposeful

*The Lord will fulfill his purpose for me; your steadfast love, O Lord, endures forever.
Do not forsake the work of your hands.*
Psalm 138:8 ESV

I am Triumphant

*Now thanks be unto God, which always causeth us to triumph in Christ, and
maketh manifest the savour of his knowledge by us in every place.*
2 Corinthians 2:14 KJV

I am Qualified

*Giving thanks to the Father, who has qualified you to share in the
inheritance of the saints in light.*
Colossians 1:12 ESV

Reflections

Prayer

I Am Unafraid

I, even I, am he that comforteth you: who art thou, that thou shouldest be afraid of a man that shall die, and of the son of man which shall be made as grass.
Isaiah 51:12 KJV

I am United with Christ

For if we have been planted together in the likeness of his death, we shall be also in the likeness of his resurrection.
Romans 6:5 KJV

I am an Ambassador

Now then we are ambassadors for Christ, as though God did beseech you by us: we pray you in Christ's stead, be ye reconciled to God.
2 Corinthians 5:20 KJV

Reflections

Prayer

I Am Anointed

But ye have an unction from the Holy One, and ye know all things.
1 John 2:20 KJV

I am Anxious for nothing

Be careful for nothing; but in everything by prayer and supplication with thanksgiving let your requests be made known unto God.
Philippians 4:6 KJV

I am Guided

For such is God, Our God forever and ever; He will guide us until death.
Psalm 48:14 NASB

Reflections

Prayer

I Am Guiltless

Therefore there is now no condemnation for those who are in Christ Jesus.
Romans 8:1 NASB

I am a Minister

Who also made us sufficient as ministers of the new covenant, not of the letter but of the Spirit; for the letter kills, but the Spirit gives life.
2 Corinthians 3:6 NKJV

I am the Head

The Lord will make you the head and not the tail, and you only will be above, and you will not be underneath, if you listen to the commandments of the Lord your God, which I charge you today, to observe them carefully.
Deuteronomy 28:13 NASB

Reflections

Prayer

SECTION III
Weeks 25-36

Be not conformed to this world, but be ye transformed
by the renewing of your mind.
(ROMANS 12:2)

I am a Minister of reconciliation

*Now all things are of God, who has reconciled us to Himself through Jesus Christ,
and has given us the ministry of reconciliation, [19] that is, that God was in Christ
reconciling the world to Himself, not imputing their trespasses to them,
and has committed to us the word of reconciliation.*
2 Corinthians 5:18-19 NKJV

I am Upheld

For the arms of the wicked shall be broken: but the Lord upholdeth the righteous.
Psalm 37:17 KJV

I am a Mountain mover

*So Jesus answered and said to them, "Have faith in God. For assuredly, I say to
you, whoever says to this mountain, 'Be removed and be cast into the sea,' and does not
doubt in his heart, but believes that those things he says will be done,
he will have whatever he says.*
Mark 11:22-23 NKJV

Reflections

Prayer

I am Upright

My defense is of God, which saveth the upright in heart.
Psalm 7:10 KJV

I have Understanding

Consider what I say; and the Lord give thee understanding in all things.
2 Timothy 2:7 KJV

I am Useful for His glory

Even every one that is called by my name: for I have created him for my glory, I have formed him; yea, I have made him.
Isaiah 43:7 KJV

Reflections

Prayer

I am Valuable

Consider the ravens: for they neither sow nor reap; which neither have storehouse nor barn; and God feedeth them: how much more are ye better than the fowls?
Luke 12:24 KJV

I am Victorious

But thanks be to God, which giveth us the victory through our Lord Jesus Christ.
1 Corinthians 15:57 KJV

I am Walking in His light

But if we walk in the light, as he is in the light, we have fellowship one with another, and the blood of Jesus Christ his Son cleanseth us from all sin.
1 John 1:7 KJV

Reflections

Prayer

I am the Apple of His eye

For thus saith the Lord of hosts; After the glory hath he sent me unto the nations which spoiled you: for he that toucheth you toucheth the apple of his eye.
Zechariah 2:8 KJV

I am Appointed by God

Ye have not chosen me, but I have chosen you, and ordained you, that ye should go and bring forth fruit, and that your fruit should remain: that whatsoever ye shall ask of the Father in my name, he may give it you.
John 15:16 KJV

I am the Aroma of Christ

For we are unto God a sweet savour of Christ, in them that are saved, and in them that perish.
2 Corinthians 2:15 KJV

Reflections

Prayer

Reflections

I am not Ashamed

For the which cause I also suffer these things: nevertheless I am not ashamed: for I know whom I have believed, and am persuaded that he is able to keep that which I have committed unto him against that day.
2 Timothy 1:12 KJV

I am Assured of reward

Therefore, my beloved brethren, be ye stedfast, unmoveable, always abounding in the work of the Lord, forasmuch as ye know that your labour is not in vain in the Lord.
1 Corinthians 15:58 KJV

I am Beautiful

For the Lord taketh pleasure in his people: he will beautify the meek with salvation.
Psalm 149:4 KJV

Reflections

Prayer

I am Healed

And He Himself bore our sins in His body on the cross, so that we might die to sin and live to righteousness; for by His wounds you were healed.
1 Peter 2:24 NASB

I am an Heir of God

So that being justified by His grace we would be made heirs according to the hope of eternal life.
Titus 3:7 NASB

I am a Warrior

(For the weapons of our warfare are not carnal, but mighty through God to the pulling down of strong holds;)
2 Corinthians 10:4 KJV

Reflections

Prayer

I am Washed

Not by works of righteousness which we have done, but according to his mercy he saved us, by the washing of regeneration, and renewing of the Holy Ghost.
Titus 3:5 KJV

I am Watching for His return

Blessed are those servants, whom the lord when he cometh shall find watching: verily I say unto you, that he shall gird himself, and make them to sit down to meat, and will come forth and serve them.
Luke 12:37 KJV

I am Becoming a mature person

Till we all come in the unity of the faith, and of the knowledge of the Son of God, unto a perfect man, unto the measure of the stature of the fulness of Christ.
Ephesians 4:13 KJV

Reflections

Prayer

I am God's

*I pray for them: I pray not for the world, but for them which thou
hast given me; for they are thine.*
John 17:9 KJV

I am Betrothed

*And I will betroth thee unto me forever; yea, I will betroth thee unto me in
righteousness, and in judgment, and in lovingkindness, and in mercies.*
Hosea 2:19 KJV

I am Jesus' Brother

*For both he that sanctifieth and they who are sanctified are all of one: for which cause
he is not ashamed to call them brethren.*
Hebrews 2:11 KJV

Reflections

Prayer

I am Healthy

*The Lord will remove from you all sickness; and He will not put
on you any of the harmful diseases of Egypt which you have known,
but He will lay them on all who hate you.*
Deuteronomy 7:15 NASB

I am Cleansed

*If we confess our sins, he is faithful and just to forgive us our sins, and to cleanse us
from all unrighteousness.*
1 John 1:9 KJV

I am made Strong

*Therefore I take pleasure in infirmities, in reproaches, in necessities, in persecutions,
in distresses for Christ's sake: for when I am weak, then am I strong.*
2 Corinthians 12:10 KJV

Reflections

____

____

____

____

____

____

____

____

____

____

____

____

Prayer

____

____

____

____

____

Reflections

I am in a Wealthy place

Thou hast caused men to ride over our heads; we went through fire and through water: but thou broughtest us out into a wealthy place.
Psalm 66:12 KJV

I am Covered in armour

Put on the whole armour of God, that ye may be able to stand against the wiles of the devil.
Ephesians 6:11 KJV

I am made Whole

And he said unto her, Daughter, thy faith hath made thee whole; go in peace, and be whole of thy plague.
Mark 5:34 KJV

Reflections

Prayer

Reflections

I am Conformed

For whom he did foreknow, he also did predestinate to be conformed to the image of his Son, that he might be the firstborn among many brethren.
Romans 8:29 KJV

I am a Believer

That if thou shalt confess with thy mouth the Lord Jesus, and shalt believe in thine heart that God hath raised him from the dead, thou shalt be saved.
Romans 10:9 KJV

I am Hidden

For you have died and your life is hidden with Christ in God.
Colossians 3:3 NASB

Reflections

Prayer

I am Near to God

*But now in Christ Jesus you who once were far off have been
brought near by the blood of Christ.*
Ephesians 2:13 NKJV

I am Wise

For the Lord giveth wisdom: out of his mouth cometh knowledge and understanding.
Proverbs 2:6 KJV

I am His Witness

*But ye shall receive power, after that the Holy Ghost is come upon you: and ye shall
be witnesses unto me both in Jerusalem, and in all Judaea, and in Samaria,
and unto the uttermost part of the earth.*
Acts 1:8 KJV

Reflections

Prayer

Reflections

SECTION IV
Weeks 37-48

We are made in God's image.
(GENESIS 1:27)

I am Blameless

*Who shall also confirm you unto the end, that ye may be blameless
in the day of our Lord Jesus Christ.*
1 Corinthians 1:8 KJV

I am Blessed

*Blessed be the God and Father of our Lord Jesus Christ, who hath blessed us with
all spiritual blessings in heavenly places in Christ.*
Ephesians 1:3 KJV

I am His Handiwork

*For we are His workmanship, created in Christ Jesus for good works, which God
prepared beforehand so that we would walk in them.*
Ephesians 2:10 NASB

Reflections

Prayer

I am Holy

Just as He chose us in Him before the foundation of the world, that we would be holy and blameless before Him in love.
Ephesians 1:4 NASB

I am not of this World

I have given them thy word; and the world hath hated them, because they are not of the world, even as I am not of the world.
John 17:14 KJV

I am Yielded to God

Neither yield ye your members as instruments of unrighteousness unto sin: but yield yourselves unto God, as those that are alive from the dead, and your members as instruments of righteousness unto God.
Romans 6:13 KJV

Reflections

Prayer

I am Heaven bound

*To an inheritance incorruptible, and undefiled, and that fadeth not away,
reserved in heaven for you.*
1 Peter 1:4 KJV

I am a Worshipper

O come, let us worship and bow down: let us kneel before the Lord our maker.
Psalm 95:6 KJV

I am Honored

*Therefore, if anyone cleanses himself from these things, he will be a vessel for honor,
sanctified, useful to the Master, prepared for every good work.*
2 Timothy 2:21 NASB

Reflections

Prayer

Reflections

I am the Image of God

*God created man in His own image, in the image of God He created him;
male and female He created them.*
Genesis 1:27 NASB

I am Worthy

*Thou hast a few names even in Sardis which have not defiled their garments; and they
shall walk with me in white: for they are worthy.*
Revelation 3:4 KJV

I am Yoked with Jesus

*Take my yoke upon you, and learn of me; for I am meek and lowly in heart:
and ye shall find rest unto your souls.*
Matthew 11:29 KJV

Reflections

Prayer

Reflections

I am never Forsaken

Let your conduct be without covetousness; be content with such things as you have.
For He Himself has said, "I will never leave you nor forsake you."
Hebrews 13:5 NKJV

I am New

And that you put on the new man which was created according to God,
in true righteousness and holiness.
Ephesians 4:24 NKJV

I am Blood bought

What? know ye not that your body is the temple of the Holy Ghost which is in you,
which ye have of God, and ye are not your own?
1 Corinthians 6:19 KJV

Reflections

Prayer

I am Bold

The wicked flee when no man pursueth: but the righteous are bold as a lion.
Proverbs 28:1 KJV

I am Circumcised

In whom also ye are circumcised with the circumcision made without hands, in putting off the body of the sins of the flesh by the circumcision of Christ.
Colossians 2:11 KJV

I am a Bond servant

O Lord, truly I am thy servant; I am thy servant, and the son of thine handmaid: thou hast loosed my bonds.
Psalm 116:16 KJV

Reflections

Prayer

I am Born again

*Being born again, not of corruptible seed, but of incorruptible,
by the word of God, which liveth and abideth for ever.*
1 Peter 1:23 KJV

I am Dead in Christ

*Therefore we are buried with him by baptism into death: that like as
Christ was raised up from the dead by the glory of the Father,
even so we also should walk in newness of life.*
Romans 6:4 KJV

I am Encouraged

*Now our Lord Jesus Christ himself, and God, even our Father, which hath loved us, and
hath given us everlasting consolation and good hope through grace, Comfort your hearts,
and stablish you in every good word and work.*
2 Thessalonians 2:16-17 KJV

Reflections

Prayer

I am Born of God

*We know that whosoever is born of God sinneth not; but he that is begotten of God
keepeth himself, and that wicked one toucheth him not.*
1 John 5:18 KJV

I am Called

*But the God of all grace, who hath called us unto his eternal glory by Christ Jesus,
after that ye have suffered a while, make you perfect, stablish, strengthen, settle you.*
1 Peter 5:10 KJV

I am Raised up with Christ

*And raised us up with him and seated us with him
in the heavenly places in Christ Jesus.*
Ephesians 2:6 ESV

Reflections

Prayer

Reflections

I am a Slave to righteousness

And, having been set free from sin, have become slaves of righteousness.
Romans 6:18 ESV

I am Bought with a price

For ye are bought with a price: therefore glorify
God in your body, and in your spirit, which are God's.
1 Corinthians 6:20 KJV

I am a Citizen of Heaven

For our conversation is in heaven; from whence also we look for
the Saviour, the Lord Jesus Christ.
Philippians 3:20 KJV

Reflections

Prayer

I am the Glory of God

For a man ought not to have his head covered, since he is the image and glory of God.
1 Corinthians 11:7 NASB

I am an Imitator of God

Therefore be imitators of God, as beloved children.
Ephesians 5:1 NASB

I am a Newborn

As newborn babes, desire the pure milk of the word, that you may grow thereby.
1 Peter 2:2 NKJV

Reflections

Prayer

I am Clay

O house of Israel, cannot I do with you as this potter? saith the Lord. Behold, as the clay is in the potter's hand, so are ye in mine hand, O house of Israel.
Jeremiah 18:6 KJV

I am Walking in a new life

Therefore we were buried with Him through baptism into death, that just as Christ was raised from the dead by the glory of the Father, even so we also should walk in newness of life.
Romans 6:4 NKJV

I am a Branch of the true vine

I am the vine, ye are the branches: He that abideth in me, and I in him, the same bringeth forth much fruit: for without me ye can do nothing.
John 15:5 KJV

Reflections

____

____

____

____

____

____

____

____

____

____

____

Prayer

____

____

____

____

____

Reflections

I am Indestructible

I am the living bread that came down out of heaven; if anyone eats of this bread, he will live forever; and the bread also which I will give for the life of the world is My flesh.
John 6:51 KJV

I am Cared for

Casting all your care upon him; for he careth for you.
1 Peter 5:7 KJV

I am Chosen

But ye are a chosen generation, a royal priesthood, an holy nation, a peculiar people; that ye should shew forth the praises of him who hath called you out of darkness into his marvellous light.
1 Peter 2:9 KJV

Reflections

Prayer

SECTION V
Weeks 49-60

Be still and know that I am God.
(PSALM 46:10)

I am Cherished

For no man ever yet hated his own flesh; but nourisheth and cherisheth it,
even as the Lord the church.
Ephesians 5:29 KJV

I am Renewed

So we do not lose heart. Though our outer self is wasting away, our
inner self is being renewed day by day.
2 Corinthians 4:16 ESV

I am Complete in Christ

And ye are complete in him, which is the head of all principality and power.
Colossians 2:10 KJV

Reflections

Prayer

I am in Christ Jesus

But by His doing you are in Christ Jesus, who became to us wisdom from God, and righteousness and sanctification, and redemption.
1 Corinthians 1:30 NASB

I am an Instrument of righteousness

And do not go on presenting the members of your body to sin as instruments of unrighteousness; but present yourselves to God as those alive from the dead, and your members as instruments of righteousness to God.
Romans 6:13 NASB

I am a New Creation

Therefore, if anyone is in Christ, he is a new creation; old things have passed away; behold, all things have become new.
2 Corinthians 5:17 NKJV

Reflections

Prayer

I am not a Slave to Sin

Knowing this, that our old man was crucified with Him, that the body of sin might be done away with, that we should no longer be slaves of sin.
Romans 6:6 NKJV

I am Rescued

He has delivered us from the domain of darkness and transferred us to the kingdom of his beloved Son.
Colossians 1:13 ESV

I am Reconciled to God

For if while we were enemies we were reconciled to God by the death of his Son, much more, now that we are reconciled, shall we be saved by his life.
Romans 5:10 ESV

Reflections

Prayer

I am Redeemed

Christ redeemed us from the curse of the law by becoming a curse for us—for it is written, "Cursed is everyone who is hanged on a tree".
Galatians 3:13 ESV

I am Calm

Be careful for nothing; but in everything by prayer and supplication with thanksgiving let your requests be made known unto God.
Philippians 4:6 KJV

I am Reigning with Christ

For if, because of one man's trespass, death reigned through that one man, much more will those who receive the abundance of grace and the free gift of righteousness reign in life through the one man Jesus Christ.
Romans 5:17 ESV

Reflections

Prayer

I am Empowered

For it is God which worketh in you both to will and to do of his good pleasure.
Philippians 2:13 KJV

I am Confident

Herein is our love made perfect, that we may have boldness in the day of judgment: because as he is, so are we in this world.
1 John 4:17 KJV

I am Courageous

And David said to Solomon his son, Be strong and of good courage, and do it: fear not, nor be dismayed: for the Lord God, even my God, will be with thee; he will not fail thee, nor forsake thee, until thou hast finished all the work for the service of the house of the Lord.
1 Chronicles 28:20 KJV

Reflections

Prayer

Reflections

I am Safe

In peace I will both lie down and sleep; for you alone,
O Lord, make me dwell in safety.
Psalm 4:8 ESV

I am Indwelt by Christ

In that day you will know that I am in My Father,
and you in Me, and I in you.
John 14:20 NASB

I am Inseparable from His Love

Who will separate us from the love of Christ? Will tribulation, or distress, or
persecution, or famine, or nakedness, or peril, or sword?
Romans 8:35 NASB

Reflections

Prayer

Reflections

I am Led in triumph

But thanks be to God, who always leads us in triumph in Christ, and manifests
through us the sweet aroma of the knowledge of Him in every place.
2 Corinthians 2:14 NASB

I am an Overcomer

For whatever is born of God overcomes the world. And this is the victory that has
overcome the world— our faith. Who is he who overcomes the world, but he who believes
that Jesus is the Son of God?
1 John 5:4-5 NKJV

I am a Partaker of Christ

For we have become partakers of Christ if we hold the beginning of
our confidence steadfast to the end.
Hebrews 3:14 NKJV

Reflections

Prayer

Reflections

I am full of God's Peace

And the peace of God, which surpasses all understanding, will guard your hearts and minds through Christ Jesus.
Philippians 4:7 NKJV

I am in an unshakeable kingdom

Therefore let us be grateful for receiving a kingdom that cannot be shaken, and thus let us offer to God acceptable worship, with reverence and awe.
Hebrews 12:28 ESV

I am Rich

For you know the grace of our Lord Jesus Christ, that though he was rich, yet for your sake he became poor, so that you by his poverty might become rich.
2 Corinthians 8:9 ESV

Reflections

Prayer

Reflections

I am Saved

*For by grace you have been saved through faith. And this is
not your own doing; it is the gift of God.*
Ephesians 2:8 ESV

I am Brought near

*But now in Christ Jesus ye who sometimes were far off
are made nigh by the blood of Christ.*
Ephesians 2:13 KJV

I am Santified

*And such were some of you. But you were washed, you were sanctified, you were
justified in the name of the Lord Jesus Christ and by the Spirit of our God.*
1 Corinthians 6:11 ESV

Reflections

Prayer

I am Created in His image

*So God created man in his own image, in the image of God created he him;
male and female created he them.*
Genesis 1:27 KJV

I am Dead to sin

*Likewise reckon ye also yourselves to be dead indeed unto sin, but alive unto God
through Jesus Christ our Lord.*
Romans 6:11 KJV

I am Indwelt by the Holy Spirit

*But if the Spirit of Him who raised Jesus from the dead dwells in you, He who raised
Christ Jesus from the dead will also give life to your mortal bodies
through His Spirit who dwells in you.*
Romans 8:11 NASB

Reflections

Prayer

I am Joyful

Rejoice in the Lord always; again I will say, rejoice!
Philippians 4:4 NASB

I am filled with Wisdom

But if any of you lacks wisdom, let him ask of God, who gives to all generously and without reproach, and it will be given to him.
James 1:5 NASB

I am Predestined

In Him also we have obtained an inheritance, being predestined according to the purpose of Him who works all things according to the counsel of His will.
Ephesians 1:11 NKJV

Reflections

Prayer

I am Patient

You also be patient. Establish your hearts, for the coming of the Lord is at hand.
James 5:8 NKJV

I am Seated with Christ

*And raised us up with him and seated us with him in
the heavenly places in Christ Jesus.*
Ephesians 2:6 9 ESV

I am Royalty

*The Spirit himself bears witness with our spirit that we are children of God, and if
children, then heirs—heirs of God and fellow heirs with Christ, provided we suffer with
him in order that we may also be glorified with him.*
Romans 8:16-17 KJV

Reflections

Prayer

PAY IT FORWARD

Want an opportunity to share your faith and message of Christ through the written word, throughout the world?

Christians can demonstrate to the world how real and alive their God is through the reflections and prayers they've written in WHO I AM: REBORN AND CERTIFIED IN CHRIST interactive devotional.

We invite every Christian to a time of prayer and worship with the Lord by going through the WHO I AM book for a minimum of 20 weeks.

Register with JLHolman publisher to have an opportunity to get your reflections and/or prayers included in the **2020 Pay It Forward** book for FREE!

To register (for FREE) your acceptance of this invite, email us at payitforward@jlholman.com.

Go to www.jlholman.com for details about this exciting program.

(This program is only available through 2019.)

ABOUT THE AUTHOR

Terry Nichols-Alexander was born in Chicago, Illinois, and in July 2007 she became a licensed minister through Abundant Life Christian Center Fellowship, in Northern California. Her mission is to help the body of Christ become aware of their spiritual reality.

The most profound experience for Terry was when she worked in San Francisco, as a chef, in one of the largest homeless shelters in the Bay Area. Being in contact with people daily who needed love and just simple companionship was an amazing experience for her. Being able to minister the Word of God to those who needed truth, encouragement, and inspiration was a tremendous blessing to her. Today, she is still in touch with a few of the shelter's clients, who either gave or rededicated their lives to Christ.

One of her volunteers wanted to begin a ministry of purpose. So, PurpMe was established. She was honored to have been able to encourage the young man to establish the ministry. The ministry has traveled to various parts of Egypt to serve the people of small townships with food, clean water and the Word of God!

Terry takes every opportunity to introduce people to Jesus. She continues her journey, despite hindrances or delays, to help people discover their spiritual identity in Christ Jesus.

She currently resides in Clinton, Mississippi, helping to care for her mother.

If your life has been impacted by this book, please let us know. We want to hear from you.

We look forward to hearing your testimonies!

Contact us at terryalexander@jlholman.com

To order additional copies of this book, go to Amazon.com. For bulk orders, contact us at bookorders@jlholman.com or mail request to:

JL Holman
Publishers
P.O. Box 6602
Visalia, CA 93290